Haiku U.

Haiku U.

From Aristotle to Zola,
100 Great Books in 17 Syllables

David M. Bader

GOTHAM BOOKS

GOTHAM BOOKS
Published by Penguin Group (USA) Inc.
375 Hudson Street, New York, New York 10014, U.S.A.
Penguin Group (Canada), 10 Alcorn Avenue, Toronto, Ontario, Canada M4V 3B2 (a division of
Pearson Penguin Canada Inc.); Penguin Books Ltd, 80 Strand, London WC2R 0RL, England;
Penguin Ireland, 25 St Stephen's Green, Dublin 2, Ireland (a division of Penguin Books Ltd);
Penguin Group (Australia), 250 Camberwell Road, Camberwell, Victoria 3124, Australia (a divi-
sion of Pearson Australia Group Pty Ltd); Penguin Books India Pvt Ltd, 11 Community Centre,
Panchsheel Park, New Delhi - 110 017, India; Penguin Group (NZ), cnr Airborne and Rosedale
Roads, Albany, Auckland 1310, New Zealand (a division of Pearson New Zealand Ltd); Penguin
Books (South Africa) (Pty) Ltd, 24 Sturdee Avenue, Rosebank, Johannesburg 2196, South Africa

Penguin Books Ltd, Registered Offices: 80 Strand, London WC2R 0RL, England

Published by Gotham Books, a division of Penguin Group (USA) Inc.

First printing, April 2005

10 9 8 7 6 5 4 3 2 1

Copyright © 2005 by David M. Bader

Gotham Books and the skyscraper logo are trademarks of Penguin Group (USA) Inc.

LIBRARY OF CONGRESS CATALOGING-IN-PUBLICATION DATA
Bader, David. M.
    Haiku U. : from Aristotle to Zola, 100 great books in 17 syllables / David M. Bader.
        p. cm.
    ISBN 1-592-40128-7 (alk. paper)
1. Haiku—Humor. 2. Books—Humor. I. Title: Haiku U. II. Title.
PN6231.H28B34   2005
811'.54—dc22   2004029325

Printed in the United States of America

Set in Weiss with Present display • Designed by Sabrina Bowers
Illustrations by Vicki Vebell/Artworks Illustration

This book is printed on acid-free paper. ∞

Acknowledgments

The author thanks the many people who helped him condense, edit, and trample the great books into 17 syllables: Erin Moore of Gotham Books; literary agents John Boswell, Lauren Galit, and Christa Bourg; Valerie Stanford, who was a willing human test subject for a number of these haiku; and bibliophile and attorney-at-law Benjamin E. Rosenberg, Esq., who generously contributed many useful suggestions without even billing for his time. The author also thanks his parents, whose love and encouragement over the years helped him become educated way beyond his intelligence. Most of all, the author acknowledges his debt to the towering writers and thinkers who inspired this book. He takes full blame for all mistakes, except when it is obviously their fault.

Foreword

In the fifteenth century, Gutenberg's movable-type printing press revolutionized the world of publishing. Previously, books had been so scarce that it was not uncommon for a library to have only a handful of bound Latin manuscripts, chained to a desk. Beach reading was rare and required furniture movers. After Gutenberg, millions of books on all subjects were published, some of them highly influential, "great," or at least very long.

This in turn led to eyestrain, paper cuts, deforestation, and adult reading groups.

In Japan, meanwhile, the seventeen-syllable haiku began to emerge. Developed by Zen monks possibly suffering from attention deficit disorder, these poems were packed with keen insights on frogs and cherry blossoms yet short enough to be recited in a single breath. Japanese readers could experience and savor the finest haiku of Bashō in its entirety (three lines), while Western readers of, say, John Milton's *Paradise Lost* (10,000 lines) were still staring at the title page.

This collection attempts to combine these two breakthroughs. Condensed into haiku, the "great books" are now within reach of even the shortest attention spans. The formal requirements of haiku (three lines of five, seven, and five syllables, respectively) have, admittedly, made it necessary to cut some things, such as characters, plot, dialogue, and descriptive passages. Still, these are small sacrifices in view of the huge savings in time and shelf space. As an added benefit, when asked, "Did you really get all the way through *War and Peace?*" readers can now suavely reply, "No, but I read the haiku."

Deciding which books to include was difficult, as there were so many worthy candidates. In the end, selections were made on the basis of a scientific formula that took into consideration historical importance, originality, weight (in hardcover), and impact on the reader (both as a book and as a sedative). The result is this set of one hundred haiku, designed to be read and enjoyed without interfering with anyone's weekend plans. At the end, there will not be a quiz.

Geoffrey Chaucer

The Canterbury Tales

Pilgrimmes on spryng braecke—

  roadde trippe! Whoe farrtted? Yiuw didde.

  Noe, naught meae. Yaes, yiuw.

Homer

The Iliad

Sing, Goddess, of how
    brooding Achilles' mood swings
        caused him to act out.

Haiku U.

Sophocles

Oedipus Rex

Chorus: Poor bastard.

Oedipus: This is awful!

Blind Seer: Told you so.

Marcel Proust

Remembrance of Things Past

Tea-soaked madeleine—
a childhood recalled. I had
brownies like that once.

Plato

Phaedo

By Zeus, Socrates!

It seems you're right once again!

Time for your hemlock.

Homer

The Odyssey

Aegean forecast—
storms, chance of one-eyed giants,
delays expected.

Nicolaus Copernicus

De Revolutionibus Orbium Cælestium

Guessus whatibus?

Earthus orbits the Sunnum!

Ptolemy doofus.

Beowulf

Hrothgar's hall,   haunted.
    Dauntless Danes die,   Grendel-gored.
        Why not   hrelocate?

Marcus Aurelius

Meditations

As grapes become wine,

so must one accept one's fate.

Die well. Like a grape.

Dante Alighieri

The Inferno

Abandon all hope!
Looks like everyone's down here.
Omigod—the Pope!

Herman Melville

Moby-Dick

Vengeance! Black blood! Aye!
Doubloons to him that harpoons
the Greenpeace dinghy.

St. Augustine

The Confessions

This is just to say

I screwed around. Forgive me.

I enjoyed it so.

Jane Austen

Pride and Prejudice

Single white lass seeks
landed gent for marriage, whist.
No parsons, thank you.

Charles Dickens

Bleak House

Fog, gloom, men in wigs—
the Chancery Court blights all.
See where law school leads?

Niccolò Machiavelli

The Prince

What I learned at court:

Being more feared than loved—good.

Getting poisoned—bad.

René Descartes

Discourse on Method

If I think, I am.
If I don't exist, how do
I know about me?

Samuel Richardson

Clarissa, or, The History of a Young Lady: Comprehending the Most Important Concerns of Private Life, and Particularly Showing the Distresses That May Attend the Misconduct Both of Parents and Children, in Relation to Marriage

To Miss Howe: Send help!
I've been raped in Volume Six
with three more to go.

Isaac Newton

Philosophiae Naturalis
Principia Mathematica

Cherry blossoms fall
with Force equal to Mass times
Acceleration.

Albert Einstein

Relativity: The Special and General Theory

Cherry blossoms fall
at light speed through curved space-time
and land with a thud.

Daniel Defoe

Robinson Crusoe

Alone for twelve years,
   then a footprint in the sand.
      Thank God! A servant!

Adam Smith

The Wealth of Nations

Supply meets demand.
The invisible hand claps.
Capitalist Zen.

Karl Marx

Das Kapital

October winds blow.
Your contradictions doom you,
capitalist swine.

Gustave Flaubert

Madame Bovary

Poor foolish Emma,

ruined by romance novels.

Could haiku have helped?

Herodotus

The Histories

Go tell the Spartans—
     the Persian hordes are fierce and
          wear funny slippers.

Jonathan Swift

Gulliver's Travels

Thus I was first great,
then small, and much vexed to learn
that size *does* matter.

Louisa May Alcott

Little Women

Snow-drops hang like tears.
Shy, sweet, saintly Beth has died.
One down, three to go.

Thomas Paine

Common Sense

Fellow patriots,

wake up and smell the taxed tea.

Independence now!

Alexandre Dumas

The Count of Monte Cristo

Gallant avenger.
Egg-dipped cheese sandwich. Thy name
is Monte Cristo.

Samuel Beckett

Waiting for Godot

Act I. "It's hopeless.

My boots don't fit. Where is God?"

Act II. The same thing.

Evelyn Waugh

Brideshead Revisited

Gay Anglo-Catholics—
what else to expect from a
man named Evelyn?

Miguel de Cervantes

Don Quixote

Dusk—the windmills turn.
Is the Don mad, or are we?
No, it's him all right.

William Shakespeare

Hamlet

"His mother wed his
       dead murdered father's brother!"
              Next Jerry Springer.

Nathaniel Hawthorne

The Scarlet Letter

Grim, gray New England—
all adulterers receive
free monogramming.

Aristotle

Metaphysics

Substance has essence.

Form adds whatness to thatness.

Whatsits have thinghood.

Voltaire

Candide, or, Optimism

A naive young man
learns that bad things do happen
to smug *philosophes*.

Emily Brontë

Wuthering Heights

Wild. Strange. A bit damp.
Heathcliff waits for Cathy's ghost.
Women. Always late.

Francis Parkman

The Oregon Trail

Fresh from Harvard Law,
    I went west. Sioux Indians?
        I thought they said "sue."

37

D. H. Lawrence

Lady Chatterley's Lover

On the grounds, fresh game.
On the new gamekeeper, fresh
Lady Chatterley.

Upton Sinclair

The Jungle

Slaughterhouse karma—
the dying ox returns as
Durham's Potted Meat.

Edward Gibbon

The History of the Decline and Fall of the Roman Empire

From[1] rule[2] to[3] ruin[4].

Rome's[5] last[6] words[7]: "Help! I've fallen and I can't get up."[8]

---

1. Tertullian, *Apol.* c. 6, p.80.

2. In the second century of the Christian Era, this ancient and renowned power, the *Imperium Romanum, amplitudo quae fuit Roma*—you know, Rome—held dominion over lands spanning three continents, from oceanfront property in Spain to valuable time-shares in the Euphrates valley, its gentle yet powerful influence comprehending the most civilized portion of mankind and most of the best restaurants.

3. Pliny the Elder, *Hist. Natur.* l. vi. c. 32. Also Pliny the Younger, *Letters.* vi., xiv. In fact, the whole Pliny family agrees on this.

4. For such was its state when Rome, suffering from its own immoderate greatness, its aims achieved by conquest undone by misrule, its martial spirit enfeebled by religion, its defenses breached by barbarism, its head throbbing and its tongue fuzzy from a major post-orgy hangover, moaned, staggered a few steps, and just keeled over. For more on the orgies, see Lacivius, *De Perversitate* (Leyden ed.).

5. See fn. 2, *supra*. Seven hills, all roads lead to it, gladiators. Enough said.

6. The sedulous reader, feeling the exasperation of a long journey whose destination seems ever out of reach, anticipating that the attainment of the goal may require some fortifying infusion, following the example of the author who, himself, has needed a bracing libation on not a few occasions, particularly during his digression on Bulgarian armaments, may here find it salutary to avail himself of the revivifying powers of spirits, perhaps a double.

7. For a few words on the decline of the Eastern Empire and the career of Mahomet, including his summer jobs, see Volumes V–VI.

8. *"Succurre! Cecidi nec surgere possum."*

Honoré de Balzac

Old Goriot

His two spoiled daughters—
they don't write, they don't visit.
This is gratitude?

Fyodor Dostoyevsky

Crime and Punishment

I, Rodya, killed her
  to prove my theory. Uh-oh.
    Back to square oneski.

Alexander Hamilton, James Madison,
John Jay

The Federalist Papers

The Constitution—

behold our work and marvel.

No Bill of Rights? Whoops.

Vladimir Nabokov

Lolita

Lecherous linguist—
    he lays low and is laid low
       after laying Lo.

Immanuel Kant

The Critique of Pure Reason

We are born knowing

circles to be circular.

We just don't know it.

Michel Foucault

Discipline and Punish:
The Birth of the Prison

Carceral discourse,

polyvalently deployed.

Hot air gently blows.

Edmund Burke

Reflections on the Revolution in France

Rights of man? Humbug!
And ladies? I pine for you,
Marie Antoinette.

Mary Shelley

Frankenstein

Strange and horrific—
a doctor makes a Monster
who is uninsured!

Franz Kafka

The Metamorphosis

"What have I become?"
    Uncertain, Gregor Samsa
        puts out some feelers.

George Orwell

1984

Love is a thoughtcrime.
  The Thought Police make Winston
    forget whatsername.

Georg Wilhelm Friedrich Hegel

Phenomenology of Spirit

Thesis: A whole pig.

Antithesis: Butcher shop.

Synthesis: Schnitzel.

Lady Murasaki Shikibu
The Tale of Genji

Two wives, ten consorts—
under the wisteria,
many warm futons.

James Boswell

Life of Johnson

That night, as we supped,

    he roared, "Pass the salt, blockhead."

        The great man liked me.

Charlotte Brontë

Jane Eyre

O woe! His mad wife—
in the attic! Had they but
lived together first.

Christopher Marlowe

Doctor Faustus

A scholar trades a

few fun years for endless Hell.

Math was not his field.

John Locke

Two Treatises of Government

Orange butterfly,
    you have no divine right to
        be called the "monarch."

Gabriel García Márquez

One Hundred Years
of Solitude

Plagues, incest, madness,
human pig-children. *Dios!*
Where does the time go?

Molière

Tartuffe, or, The Impostor

They try to outwit
　　a self-righteous hypocrite—
　　　　the first sitcom writ.

Thomas Malthus

An Essay on the Principle of Population

People multiply,
>food does not. The good news is
>>there are wars and plagues.

Leo Tolstoy

War and Peace

Guns roar, Russia burns.
Where's Andrey? Who is Petya?
Confused, France retreats.

Virginia Woolf

To the Lighthouse

Boy, death, art, earwig—
summer at the beach recalled,
minus some details.

Jean-Paul Sartre

Being and Nothingness

Gentle Left Bank sun—
    bluebirds chirp their empty songs.
        We are all condemned.

Sir Walter Scott

Ivanhoe

"Who dat fine knight be?"
asked the saucy Moorish wench.
"Dat be Ivan, ho."

Thomas Hardy

The Mayor of Casterbridge

Undone by his past—

he once sold his wife and child.

Nobody's perfect.

Lao Tzu

Tao Te Ching

The eternal Tao.

To know it is not to know.

What is it? Don't ask.

James Joyce

Ulysses

Like the cicada,
     Molly takes many years to
          say "Yes" to Leo.

William Faulkner

As I Lay Dying

Addie: I'm dyin'.

Darl: I'm nuts. Mules: We're drownded.

Anse: Need me some teeth.

Thomas Mann

The Magic Mountain

The TB "rest cure."
Haus Berghof. Death, Eros, and
all meals included.

Vatsayana

Kama Sutra

Advice for those in
a difficult position.
First, be flexible.

Henry David Thoreau

Walden, or, Life in the Woods

Morning: Pond-gazing.
Afternoon: Berry-picking.
What a hectic day.

George Bernard Shaw

Saint Joan

Strange girl. Hears voices.
But, by Jove, even in death
she lights up a room.

Oscar Wilde

The Importance of
Being Earnest

Earnestly posing
as Ernest, Jack learns he's named
Ernest in earnest.

Richard Wright

Native Son

Poor black man smothers
rich white girl. Needed: less hate
and safer pillows.

J. D. Salinger

The Catcher in the Rye

I flunked out again.

    Crumby prep schools. Bunch of dopes.

    Boy, I'm not kidding.

Anton Chekhov

The Cherry Orchard

Their bankrupt estate

sold to a former servant.

Nobles down, serfs up.

Charles Darwin

The Origin of Species

Galápagos finch—
the same beak as Aunt Enid's!
A theory is born.

F. Scott Fitzgerald

The Great Gatsby

Beauty to weep for—
coral, azure, apple green.
His custom-made shirts.

Jean-Jacques Rousseau

The Social Contract

All vote. All consent.

It's like a big family.

Not mine, but someone's.

Ivan Turgenev

Fathers and Sons

A nihilist dies

without having achieved much.

Mission accomplished.

Émile Zola

Nana

Paris courtesan—
    in her salon, men admire
        her French Empire chest.

Friedrich Wilhelm Nietzsche

Also Sprach Zarathustra

Kindness is weakness!
Abhor pity, worship strength!
Be an *über*-jerk!

James Joyce

Finnegans Wake

Riverrun on and
by Jaisus s'dense! Bien alors,
scribbledehobble.

John Milton

Paradise Lost

O'er and o'er God warned,
    "Eat not th' Apple!" Man dids't and
       God ballistick went.

Henry James

Portrait of a Lady

Will she inherit?
Which suitor will she marry?
When will tea be served?

William James

The Varieties of Religious Experience

Let's be pragmatic.

    Saints, monks, mystics—their faith works.

    So what if they're nuts?

Günter Grass

The Tin Drum

A shrieking, drumming
  dwarf winds up in a madhouse.
    It's a long story.

Henrik Ibsen

The Wild Duck

She has shot the duck!

No, Hedvig has shot herself.

[Offstage, relieved quacks.]

Thomas More

Utopia

An austere commune—

"Utopia." It's Greek for

"Nice, if you're a monk."

Alexis de Tocqueville

Democracy in America

So free! So un-French!
>
> We must learn from their ideas
>
> but not their cuisine.

Ayn Rand

Atlas Shrugged

One by one, tycoons
　　give up working. One by one
　　　　Dagny sleeps with them.

John Steinbeck

The Grapes of Wrath

Okie exodus—

Ma Joad's fambly keeps movin'.

Where are the darned grapes?

Johann Wolfgang von Goethe

Faust

He's damned—no, he's saved!
For German engineering,
another triumph.

Joseph Conrad

Heart of Darkness

The darkness darkened.

Oh, the horror, the horror.

It was horrible.

Sigmund Freud

The Interpretation of Dreams

Old pond. Frog jumps in.
Repressed sexual desire,
clearly Oedipal.

Carl Gustav Jung

The Archetypes and the Collective Unconscious

A patient says he
   sees the phallus of the sun.
      But then, who doesn't?

Harriet Beecher Stowe

Uncle Tom's Cabin

Goin' to glory,

Tom dies defying Legree.

He's no Uncle Tom.

Michel de Montaigne

Essays

Genteel French musings—
life, death, odd smells, my mustache.
Today's topic: Thumbs.

97

Jack London

The Call of the Wild

Alaskan tundra—
a dog finds his inner wolf.
White snows turn yellow.

George Eliot

Middlemarch

Stifling social roles,
small-town gossip—beware the
eyes of Middlemarch.

Ernest Hemingway

The Sun Also Rises

"Why can't we?" she said.

"War wound," I said. "Oy," Cohn said.

Back to Harry's Bar.